Forever Changing

Through Her Eyes

SABRINA CHANDLER

authorHOUSE®

AuthorHouse™
1663 Liberty Drive
Bloomington, IN 47403
www.authorhouse.com
Phone: 1-800-839-8640

First published by AuthorHouse   10/31/2011

ISBN: 978-1-4670-4415-8 (sc)
ISBN: 978-1-4670-4414-1 (ebk)

Library of Congress Control Number: 2011917783

Printed in the United States of America

"Can't Wait Till I Grow Up"

Life ups and downs can be so much to bear
Especially matters of the heart, always leaving a tear
Remembering as a child, you had but one care
As realized when you grow older you have many hats to wear
Some find themselves going in a circle absolutely nowhere
Like always things that happen just don't seem fair
Learning things that as a child we just weren't aware
I find my peace hearing cricket's chirp in the night air
Taking along drive letting the wind blow through my hair
Now I miss that time as a child with no worries as no peace can compare

Remembering all the things momma said, *"Be a child while you can"*

Sabrina Chandler

"They Say"

They say it was love at first sight
Couldn't have been because you didn't know them that same night
They say why purchase the cow if you can get the milk for free
I know some whose bonds are strong, and remain tight and still marry despite
They say if you don't have nothing nice to say, say nothing at all
Guess you should just front, be fake, back down, and walk away from that fight
They say you shouldn't do wrong, but it's much easier to do wrong than right
And if it's so wrong why does it feel so right
Let me interject if I might
To all this they say I say not quite
If it's not reality or fact like the sun shines bright
Or gives off a beaming light
Just saying everything they say don't always add up to right
I know what I'm saying just might bite
But hey they say everyone's entitled to their own opinion so this is my insight

"Leave Nothing Behind"

Wait one minute let me finish my glass of wine
Contrary to the thoughts running through your mind
I'm not trying to marry you or make you mine
I just want to live life, laugh, and have a good time
True you may be one of a kind and with you this maybe that one chance
in a lifetime
Right now I'm just chilling, on my grind
I'm telling you upfront, so you don't have to worry about missing no signs
Or reading between any lines
Honestly labels, relationships and marriage I wasn't looking to find
So please please take all your things and leave nothing behind

"I Can't Stop Loving Me"

Myself, I'll always treat; I'm going to get me something to eat
Drink me a glass of wine, as I dine and enjoy something sweet
Stop by the spa get me a full body massage, down to my feet
Make a quick stop at the boutique
Get my hair and nails done unique
Buy me a pair of shoes, not worried about no dudes
Not waiting for no man, he can't make me feel better about me than I can
Plan to take me a trip, buy my own new whip, Ladies allow me to give you a tip
Don't worry about what they say, if your bills they don't pay
I hold my own, and pay my own way
I have but one more thing to say
"I can't stop loving me"

"Even When"

Will you still love me if I gained a few pounds
If age dwindled my beauty would you keep me around
If times got hard would you think about the love we once found
Or will you give up because you felt you no longer wanted to be bound
If I lost my sight or couldn't hear a sound
If I contracted Alzheimer's and begin to forget simple things like coins are round
Or that a person, place, or thing is a noun
Will you still love me hold me down
Will I still wear your queen's crown?

"Loves Contrasting Nature"

Love,
Can be like the wind never knowing which way it will blow
As beautiful as a flower, but leaves the pain of its name a "bleeding heart"
Or wither away as it grows old
Change like leaves in Autumn
And lost in the Fall
Emotionally stressful and draining, like a colander
Never ending tears and stumping blocks like a running stream with layered rocks
Mountains with many peaks and heights
Confusing like a cloudy day
Why want love when love don't want you
Why love love when love don't love you
Or need you
But yet we want love for the hope that
Love,
Will stay as strong as a Pine tree never dies through the seasons,
but straw is made somehow
Remain pure, honest and true like a white dove or beautiful winter snow, but it fly's
away or may melt the same day
Bring warmth in the cold like wood in a burning fireplace,
but it burns out that same day
Overpowering like a thunderstorm, but even it comes to an end by the next day
Comfort when lonely as a bird is in its nest, but they leave anytime
within the same day
Why want love for a day's time
Why want love for a lifetime of pain and happiness that has no guarantee
Or want me
But yet I still want love for the chance that it will change and love me

? Someone to Love?

Asking myself, will I ever find someone to love?
To remain pure to me as a white dove
Be able to leave the past in past
In order to make any love last
Asking myself, will I ever find someone that's true?
Give me everything that I've given to you
Never exhibits unfaithfulness or tactics
Whose passion towards me is overwhelming automatic
Strategic and confident when it comes to me or us
Truthful, never forsaken my trust
Only sees me as I only see him
Well outlined and defined trim
Fully disclosed, not covered in wolfs clothing
As pieces of my life are unfolding
I'm asking myself, will I ever find someone?
Someone to love . . . .

"Loves Puzzle"

Love that's new, they see only you
Only when a long length of time seems like a few
A moment's time is never good enough
Before long you will be wondering, will you make it through the times
that become tough
Intrigued by curiosity and lingering for more
Hopeful the best is yet to come, anxious to see what's in store
A last glance that is hoped to last for days
Puzzling to the mind like a mice trying to make it through a maze
But should that love grow old
It will begin to grow cold leaving you wondering if the pieces will unfold

Love or Lust

Love *that's pure*
Is overpowering
Leaves you at a lost for words
Finishes statements
Knows your thoughts
Trusting, honest
Causes your heart to skip beats
Love is unconditional
Confusing, overwhelming
Causes hurt, even shed tears at times
What is love without purity, honesty, trust . . . simply hopeless
Not true Love, typically just **Lust**
Not overpowering . . . Un—happy or happy for the moment, no joy
Can't finish statements or knows your thoughts . . . . Doesn't know you
Not trusting or honest . . . Pointless
Heart don't skip beats . . . . Not mutual
Not unconditional . . . . Is not everlasting
Not confusing, overwhelming . . . . Simply doesn't care
No shedding tears or hurt . . . . Unreal (fake) simply a lie
Not True Love That's Lust

"Curiosity"

As she lies here, she wonders what is it about him that makes her smile
Why is it that when he's gone for a short time, it feels like for awhile
Curious about his love, wondering should she go the extra mile
Her heart wants to give it a go, her mind says hell no,
turning away now would be file
She likes his style, he's in her thoughts, those eyes, dimples when he halfway smile
She's confident, and knows he will be hers in a little while

"Chance"

Don't want to let go guess it's my fault since I didn't let my feelings show
Held back on letting my heart just flow
Giving up now means if there was a future we'd never know
Lets not walk away just take it slow
And see how far this may go

"Love Crazy"

Every time I say goodbye, I miss you before I blink my eye
I want to love you past your pain
Make you look forward to the rain, Feeling this way seems I'm insane
At times the way I feel about you makes me shame
In my heart for you, I carry a burning flame
But will my love be a enough to sustain? I wonder does he feel the same?

"*All of You*"

Give me all of you not just something
If I can't have all of you then I don't want anything
Though the future looks promising
You're draining my loving
Can't keep waiting while you're contemplating
Times steady wasting
If about me you're still debating my future you're delaying
I got to keep stepping
Just simply stating
I want all of you no negotiating

"*Love Cloud*"

Can't stop this smile not even for a little while
You make me want to go the extra mile
Or even think I can swim the Nile
Like when you're a kid in the candy store a young child
Your love makes me want to scream out loud
Hoping that being with me you'll always be proud
I like it here not coming down off my love cloud
You're driving me wild
Know you don't like things to spicy but our love can't be mild
Lost for words all that's left to say is wow
I still see only you in a crowd
Come on let me get it there we go almost a smile

"Contemplating"

Yet she wonders, where will it end before they start or begin
Finds comfort in his arms, overwhelmed by his charm, puzzling to the mind the
closeness felt in such short time. He gives her strength when she feels weak
Encouragement in despair; listens when she speaks
Knows the words to say to make her smile
Wondering will this last a short time or for awhile
Has her longing to have him near
Dreaming of places they could go and how the future would be to have him here

"Loves Never Belated"

Over and over about her you've contemplated
For her your loves never belated
Said you'd moved on married, but yet your heart waited
Truthfully you just made things complicated
But you see true loves never belated
Her love makes you feel elated
Peace of mind, safe vindicated
In this life places you've traded
So together love hasn't fully accelerated
Yet your love for her is overrated
So when will you get it situated
Because "True Loves Never Belated"

"Marry and be in a relationship with the one you are in love with not the one you just love then you will be able to love the one your with, and the one your with want feel that of your love they have been cheated"

"True To the Heart"

Love that can't be disclosed
Is not real, but imposed
For true love's never a secret and always shows
Trusting, even when not knowing which way the wind blows
With every moment together, your hearts already knows
Even when it's not said, it's fully disclosed
Engulfed, overwhelming true to the heart, as passion overflows

Chapter 2

"Love Life and Relations Spoken Word"

Searching for love that will stand, and not grow old. Tried to love, but her heart has endured so much pain it has grown cold. Should have thrown in the cards guess she didn't know when to fold. For love life and relations can be such a hard road. It can take such a toll through some of these writing the story of heartache is told.

"*Love Song*"

Times you've hurt me, countless
All the signs you've shown, countless
Excuses' I've made for your actions, countless
Times I've asked myself why I love you so, countless
Said I was tired but kept on trying, hoping for change, countless
Put your happiness before mine, countless
Took pride in you when others saw shame, countless
Forgiven you when I should have walked away, countless
Kept giving when there's little or nothing left to give, countless
Years I've spent waiting for you to give me the love I've given you, simply
un-retrievable
Finally you win I've had enough, you are simply unbelievable
Though all these things are about you, I ask myself

Why is finding true love so hard for me? When I give my love endlessly
Why is it my heart feels more sorrow and pain, when I give my everything
Why after all I've given, when still nothing I've gained
Why I've stayed, when given all the reasons to walk away
Why even now my heart is heavy, when still I worry if you are going to be ok
Why I question myself, when all is said and done
There's nothing left to say, again I wait for true love to come my way

Inspired By: Brandy B.

"Her Time"

As her heart grows cold and she looks up and years have gone by.
When looking back she's still at the place that she started, tears form in her eye.
She knows she can't rewind time it's just lost, but yet hopes for the brightest future,
as she tries not to cry.
When she began savoring the moments before feelings
and love changed then she sigh.
Overwhelmed with despair, emotionally distressed, Outraged from defeat,
but yet wanted to try.
When she's always promised she never try to change his mind,
but for their love hoped they'd tie.
Yet reminded him that everything has its time,
she'll grow wings as a baby bird and begin to fly.
When she's not sure why they didn't grow together,
it's like as from her love he became shy.
But knew when you don't grow together, it's the opposite,
you grow apart, she said to herself my my my.
When goodbye is hard to say, and trying seems so hard, she knows that she has
already held on too long, why?
She loves him deeply, hopes that he understands her deepest thoughts, and respects that
she didn't front or lie.
When that time comes, then will pain then will tears with both comes strength after
all, she'll remain strong, confident reborn as I.
She knows that her time is yet to come and happy tears she will then cry.

"*My My My*"

Her heart is pierced, like getting new earring, because she's hurt
Her mind is locked, like someone in jail, because she has no control
Her feelings are raging, like good and evil fighting a battle, because she's in love
Her emotions are overwhelming, though presumed calm, because they are restrained
Her body is full of anger and anguish, but still overwhelmed with passion
Her actions are innocent, though presumed guilty
Her trust in diminished, though presumed reconstructed
Her thoughts are full, though confusing, because she's unsure where you're heart and our future lies, when still she loves you.
My My My . . . . How things change but remember when
Remember when she waited for your calls, to know you were ok.
Remember when you hung out all night and she waited to feel your body heat next to her the next day.
Remember when she asked you once why your phone was always going off, though given the reason you looked like you dare to question me.
Remember when she wanted to do things but your ins and outs made her have to pick another day.
Remember when you'd get a call and secretly take a walk away.
My My My . . . . How things have changed, How tables have turned and places have changed. How naive of you to think she would always stay.

"Let Go"

*Maybe I was dreaming, my thoughts are a fairytale, make believe, seeing what I
wanted to see eyes covered by scales. Hearing what I wanted to hear,
imagining wedding bells
Trying to make this something I wanted it to be
When obliviously that ship has sailed for you and me
There was a time I saw a future and you standing next to me for life
In other words, seeing myself as your wife
But I've come to realize, just because I love you and you love me
Doesn't mean that we're meant to be
Sometimes things turnout just the way they should be
So even if the statement never becomes one or we
I accept the fact and stepped back and will always be a friend to thee.*

"Medical Emergency"

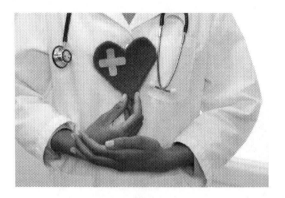

I'm gone need major surgery to remove my heart's hurt and pain
That's moved to my mind, covered by scar tissue in my brain,
in order to keep me from going insane.
From life's pitfalls and discouraging things, and constant rain
I'm surprised I still have blood running through each vein
But glad I'm not weak and somewhere high off cocaine
But I'm emotionally numb, knocked out like the anesthetic:
stovaine, mepivacaine and novocaine
In recovery, this can't be the last stop on this train
I have to be wiser and bring an end to the broken links in this chain
So in this life I'm still waiting, knowing in the end,
true love I'll surely gain

"*A Wish*"

If my wishes could come true, I'd wish to replace
Your sadness with happiness
Your rainy days with sun light
Your sorrow with joy
You're silver with gold
Your doubt restored and you believed in me and us
Your tears with a smile
Your despair with hope
Your love towards me overpowering as mines is for you
If I could only have one wish it would be to
Spend my life with you
And make you mine forever

Sabrina Chandler

"Hardest Thing"

The hardest thing about love is letting go
Even though facts are clear and you know
Holding on would just be for show
She can feel the heaviness in her heart as tears begin to flow
Wondering why she ends up in the same place many times in a row
Seems like in her life the winds are raging wishing they switch the way they blow
Reality is you should have left along time ago

???*Questions*???

Why should she stay here
What should she keep you near
Why should she even shed a tear
Why did she even love you without fear
It seems hard, but finally in life she's shifting gear
Not looking to the rear
No longer scared of starting over looking into the future to what could appear
The things that seemed cloudy but right in front of her now she sees so clear

"Lesson Learned"

Never thought that you would betray my trust for your own lust
Never thought you'd see another as you once saw me
Never thought you'd break my heart and serve it back to me
Never thought you'd break the bond we had spiritually
That enabled us to see past naturally
Infatuated by what things could be
That's what I get for not thinking clearly
It will take God to help me to forgive thee
And for it to ever be a we
God remove the scales from my eyes,
so now I can see the one that you have for me truly
One that will love you first and me habitually
God hold me in your arms so I want feel lonely as I wait
Guide me, so I want live life blindly

"Still Standing"

Thought you were my air, but I'm still breathing
Thought you were my heartbeat, but it's still beating
Thought you were my light, but I'm still gleaming
Thought you were my song, but I'm still singing
Thought you were my smile, but I'm still smiling
Thought you were my life, but I'm still living
Thought you were my dream, but I'm still dreaming
Thought it would break me, but yet I'm still standing

"Not a Total Waste"

Wish we could have found happiness together;
instead of you sacrificing yours for mine
For which, I missed all the signs
Now we depend on our love to be sorted out in time
Troubling to the heart and the mind
Not knowing where the road will end
As feelings descend
Though we both know, in each other we'll always have a friend
For your unselfishness, I must commend
Even though my heart has to mend
No one knows truly who God will send
One reason I held onto you rather than other men
Hoping it would be us in the end
But since not as lovers, at least I know I've gained a good friend

"Nothing More Than Friends"

Nothing more than friends, for years
Wiped away each others tears
Shared our deepest thoughts and fears
Can't explain this feeling, I just want you near
Change between us even noticed by our peers
I wonder can your lover see the lust in my eyes
It overcomes me even when I try to disguise
If only she knew I'd be the one she truly despise
What I'd do to lie in your arms and watch the sunrise
Sacrificing true happiness oh how he tries
Making sure over him she never cries
Covering with endless lie's
How long will it take for her to realize
Where his heart truly lie's
Our glances, too long stares and the relationship compromised
We were "Nothing more than friends for years"

Chapter 3

"Lost Spoken Word"

It is in those times when losing loved ones can be stifling and piercing to the heart, might even have broken mine. No one to talk to, for through this only God, and I can work thru. Though the fact of life is as sure as one lives one must die. Doesn't mean it won't hurt or I can't cry. There was a time that I asked myself why, but now I understand to live your life to live again. Realized one day I'll see that loved one, that true friend so for now see you later until we meet again.

"To be absent from the body is to be present with the Lord"
(KJV: II Corinthians 5:8)

"Fully Disclosed"

You are like a thief in the night
A quiet storm
Can come swift or even slow
Bring much sorrow
Leaving no choice but to let go
Breaking hearts left behind
Trouble a trying to understand mind
Leaving pain where joy once lived
Memories of what use to be
Turning smiles upside down
Making it hard to be happy
Even though it's said that's how it should be
I can't stop the tears from falling
Impact so harsh it can take your breath away
I blame you
You are <u>death,</u> well known, an un-kept secret

In Loving Memory of Vickie B. still missing you

"Until We Meet Again"

If ye are reading this then my time has come nigh.
Though you won't see me smiling, or hear me sigh.
Rests assure for in my fathers arms sleeping I lie.
For this earth was never my home I was just passing by.
For I believe faithfully in his promises, for he is God and shalt not lie.
Though I won't be standing next to you well surely meet again, so please don't cry.
Dry the tears from each weeping eye.
When that day comes I'll join you again, but in the clouds of the sky (I Thessalonians 16:17)
But until then my brethren keep the faith and keep on, praying, praising,
worshipping, and working, fight the fight, run the race, and endure
as a good soldier as did I.

Last Words: *From the beginning God chose me, (II Thessalonians 2:13)*
In return I gave my soul to thee, I chose to worship, I chose to praise, I chose to
submit, I chose to do his will for it was his destiny for me.
I chose eternal life what about you?

"Desire"

Before I leave this earth, I have but a few desires
One day, to again experience God's marvelous fire
Leave a people behind that I have been able to truly inspire
Though I have many goals, one I must acquire
As I wait patiently, with unwavering faith, doing works,
building my heavenly empire
(Don't' build your treasures on earth where your treasures
are your heart resides)
(KJV: Matthew 6:19-21)
I'll hold on to God's promises, letting the Holy Ghost be my keeper and guide, while
on my journey as a soldier wearing my full attire
(Put on your full armor of God)
(KJV: Ephesians 6:13-18)
I'll fight faithfully, endure and wait patiently, as no one knows that day or hour
Or further more when time will expire
I say to you don't get caught up waiting till you're down to the final wire
I have gratitude for God's grace, mercy and to one that would lay down his life
for me I can only admire
To reach heaven, gain eternal life is my greatest aspire

"*Simple Request*"

While I'm still here
Bring me my favorite flowers, so I can smell them
Go to my favorite restaurants, so I can get my favorite dish
and eat while I can still taste it
While I'm still here
Forgive me if I've done you wrong, so time want be wasted
Spend time with me, so with you I can say it was time well spent
Bring the kids by, so I can watch them play while I can still see,
and as they play I can still hear
If one gets hurt I can wipe their tears and pull them near
While I'm still here
Love me while I'm here, so when I've moved on great memories
you'll have of me here, even if before I left my memories weren't clear
Simply request cherish your loved ones while their still here
As one takes final rest, you'll know you did your best loving them
while they were here

Sabrina Chandler

"At Rest"

No more mourning
No more silent cries
For I'm finally at rest
This time I close my eyes . . .
No more worries
No more pain
From this I only can gain
To my family, friends, and my love be strong
And just hold on for God has never gone wrong

Chapter 4

"Losing Battle Spoken Word"

Fighting a battle in my mind like good verses evil and a race to the end of time
For which to God I lose every time
So I surrender and give an eternal yes
As there is no other or greater love than your kind.

"New Life"

As I turn this new chapter in my life, when looking back scared me
God heard my cry and drew me near,
Put his arms around me, I've gained strength and in him I have no fear
Thirsty that I may see even more clear
Praying that he will direct my path and give me understanding for what may appear
As I open my heart to him and what he has for me, I have never been more sincere

Pathway

When I was younger I had to go to church seemed like almost every weekday
Even if in the pews quietly I would play
Never understood why, but now I know for back then you planted a seed that would
soon grow and lead me the rest of the way
For in this world I would return to it if I should stray (Proverbs 22:6)
So thank you for introducing me to spirituality back in the day
I've obtained salvation and learned how essential it is to strenuously pray
Rest a sure that the seed is being nourished and made me into
the women I am today
Blessed to have you in my life and thankful to God for showing me how to express the
words my heart wants to say.
For my love and appreciation for you will never decay
Thanks for showing me the pathway and Happy Anniversary

Proverbs 22:6 KJV "Train up a child in the way he should go,
and when he is old he will not depart from it".

Inspired By: Shirley J. & Archie J.

Encouraging & Thinking

Life
At times it seems life's obstacles are hard,
but remember if there was a smooth mountain
Then we could not climb it, then how would we make it to the everlasting fountain
For if you don't tread water how will you keep from drowning
More importantly, encourage and motivate yourself,
reach even if you feel in defeat don't become droning
Nothing worth having will come easy, even if it seems easy, but very well deceiving
(Always a price)
Even Jesus died to his flesh, as so shall we though it may not be pleasing
(Die to the flesh daily)
For isn't eternal life well worth receiving?
If in your life the wind never was shifting
How would you learn to stand and appreciate when it stops blowing
In essences of your groaning, moaning, hurting or even despairing
Even if you found yourself falling
The key is to get back up, try again, and take a start at a new beginning
For your name, even yet, God has not stopped calling
(But yet I still hear you calling my name)
This is your book, you write the ending
Where will your soul find final resting?
As for me, even through life's obstacles, I'll be found rejoicing and still praising
For if it wasn't for what you've gone through, you couldn't appreciate how far
you've come, or where you're going
This is just a little something encouraging, motivating, and to get you thinking
Remembering even your life has a meaning
So don't give up keep fighting.

Inspired By: MTOP

"Friends Prayer"

Pull up a chair, relax, lean back I'd like to chat with you if I may
As I listen to you from day to day
Here are a few things that for you I kneel down and pray
That you continue to let God use you by uplifting others,
by having encouraging words to say
Though we may not know his plan, but you continue to yield and
allow him the right of way
And in his will you'll always stay
As you continue to stand strong for others he holds you in his arms,
strengthen you everyday
That God's blessings continue to descend down upon you many more years,
but especially on today.

Happy Birthday

"Remembering our fathers a prayer, call away,
we can rest knowing that everything's okay"
(KJV: James 5:16)

"Thankfully"

"New Life, New Leaf, New Chapter"

I have a hunger burning inside of me for God; I've become very <u>thirsty</u>
I want it all right now, but I know I must wait patiently
As God opens up new doors, and a new world to me "spirituality"
To see beyond naturally, and humanly
Now that's enough about me
After all it's not my anniversary
You've come into my life so recently
I'm blessed to have you and your love abundantly
Forever thankful that God used you to reach me
Grateful that he even heard my plea
Gave me a chance at life eternally
For he saw something in me that even I could not see
All the time I have spent with you thus far has been heavenly
However at times I must say pleasantry
For even when you speak/teach you reiterate for your life God's got a <u>destiny</u>
("God's got destiny on my life": Direct quote reminder)
I've gained a chance at eternal life and, for that only my soul can repay the fee
So thank you kindly
For your sacrifice, and allowing God to use you, so graciously
I'm forever grateful to have this opportunity
Through you both God has changed my life significantly
So if ever you wonder, or when you ask, if you have been able to change lives, save
souls coming from me
I must say defiantly
So when God places that Crown upon your heads of royalty
And he says "Well done my faithful servants" Know I'm going to be there to see
As I will also serve him faithfully
Though I could go on since God allows words to flow through me so freely
I'm just going to end by asking God to forevermore keep blessing MTOP <u>ministry</u>
One more thing before I go thank you to the MTOP church family
For your love, prayers support and encouragement, but lastly
*But not the least to the **Angels** of this house **"Happy Anniversary"***
For you're a blessing in me and my son's, life truly.
***FYI:** Oh if you guys decided to share this "Some of those in the congregation may*
be lost, but as you say so well Pastor and AP tell them "They'll get it tomorrow
<u>respectfully</u>".*

Faithfully yours,

Inspired By: MTOP

"Under Attack"

Satan has tried to siffle me like wheat
Determined through trails and tribulations, I'll make it over the mountain peak
Though at times I'm weary, and may feel weak
Equipped with your armor, so him I can defeat
Yet still, your face I will still seek
As I know you're my strength and will carry me from week to week
Yet I'll still praise you: waiting, humbled, and meek

"Watching Over Me"

Glad that I serve a God that sits high and looks low
Keeping me on the right path and showing me which way to go
Even if I fall or stray, he still loves me so
If temped by flesh, I can hear him clearly say no no
Watching and speaking into my life, saying not so
If I want something, he doesn't hesitate to say no, however
it's still good to have his favor though
That's for sure, trust me I know

"Glad I Found You"

It was years before I met you in that old secret place
It wasn't until then that I was saved by your grace
That I experienced joy, peace, true happiness, and true purpose found and
life wasn't a waste
It was then, when all voids were filled as your love, I fully embraced.
I can't chat with you, or track you by the natural way of Face book, MySpace, or
Twitter as the connection and communication line of prayer is far much greater.
No technical difficulties, or down wires to replace.
No modern voicemail messaging to playback, or erase. For you never miss my call,
you're always there in that old secret place.
So I'll continue to seek your face with your guidance I know I'll win this race.
Glad that after my soul you chased, for without you this life would be a lost case.

"Wait on you"

Every time I step out and start searching and doing things on my own
I mess up, fall into traps that the enemy set, and everything just goes wrong
Impatient, wanting what I think is best
Again that's when I fail every test
Causing myself more heartache and pain
Because I want things right now just to change
I finally realized that I need you in everything I do
So now I'm tired of going through
I've done things the hard way trial and error
Now I've learned and know I have to just wait on you

"I Know a Man"

Part 1

Show me a man who says his love great
I'll tell you of one who's love is greater
Whom would lie down his life for a friend that's even better
Show me a man full of lies and deceit
I'll tell you of a man that can't lie, but will wipe away your tears as you weep
Show me a man that promises he'll never leave
I'll tell you a man who will never leave or forsake you, who will truly be there when
you need, help you to succeed one you can believe
Show me a man who won't betray you because of his own lust
I'll tell you of a man you can truly trust
I know a man his name is Jesus

Part 2

You've shown me a man of this world
I've told you of one who can mold you a man
According to God's plan
Whom first loves Him then he'll know how to love you
Though he won't be perfect, but striving for perfection
Headed in the right direction

"His Love"

In you I see a man with such strength and integrity
I'm willing to wait; trust and know my sincerity
As we are bonded by fate, faith and even more through Gods clarity
Curious of the future, since we are not who we'd chose normally
Rest assure, I long and await for the day you ask for my hand formally
Though now we love, through Him we will love more abundantly

"Fully Surrendered"

I love the fact that I'm the air you breathe
Why? Besides God, I'm everything that you'll ever need
Even you know already I'm the last of a dying breed
The love that we have has no choice but be
In my heart I know that we will succeed
As we return back to our naturally sowed seed
Thankful glad God favored me, and did not base it on creed
For He put together a man made just for me, for that I'm grateful and pleased
For Gods love I'm' greedy and yours I find myself in greed
Overwhelmed that I'm loved just for being me
From both of you, your love and strength I'll feed
As the days go by, I become even more thirsty
God's given me something for money could never buy or repay the fee
And everything I've asked for you've given to me
Since I aim to please God I give my soul to thee

"*Changing*"

Life's changing for the better
Ready go ahead and release the lever
Won't stop or give up never
As my mind turns becoming even more clever
Making it well known like a bulletin header
Stand no matter the weather
As now my worries are light as a feather
God's mended a heart that was severed

"Day to Day"

Days' knowing how hard you tried to please God everyday
How you pressed your way in on Sunday
Watched as you changed and begin to follow the right way
It was you who held my hand and taught me how to call out and pray
Know I'll see you in heaven one day
Something that carries me thru each weekday, Saturday and Sunday
But as for today I'll love thru life's changes, trails
and tribulations just the same from day to day

"Vow to Love"

For so long I've waited for this day
As I search my heart for the right words to say
First and foremost I give thanks to God for hearing me when I pray
For giving us the strength to do things the right way
In His will we'll always stay
He has given me the desires of my heart and led you my way
Given us a bond spiritually and molded us like clay
And a fee only giving my soul can repay
Your trust, love, and heart I'll never betray
I'll stand beside you thru the good, and bad showing you unconditional love
that will never sway

"Once Told"

Watch your friends, the ones which you can't stop hanging
Let go of that man of the world you're chasing
You'll never know which way he's thinking
So are you truly trying to change? Or does your mind keep changing,
so with God you keep shifting
This is no game you're just playing, but a choice of where your soul
will be eternally laying
Once told, you're going to pull them, or they'll pull you in,
suddenly you find yourself sinking
So the battle you are fighting, you may very well end up losing,
in other words not winning
Just may fall back in the enemies trap, into a world of sinning
Having to start back over from the beginning
Can't say you weren't once told so choose your ending

"Missed You"

At times growing up, she wondered where he was at
But knew he was living because of a monthly check
Told many stories, haven't truly found the truth yet
Seems now they're strangers, but at least they finally met
Now for not being there everyday he seems to regret
For which honestly she forgives him, but can't forget
Found that if she didn't want to be owned by it
and wants her farther to forgive her
she had to do both forgive and forget (Matt 6:14-15)
So finally truthfully in her heart and mind she let go of it
As she sits by the window watching the sunset

"*More and More*"

I can hear the thunder roar
Lets me know soon your rains going to pour
When you rain on me I soar
And of you I want more and more
Seems I'm against the world, spirits
and principalities I'm at war (Ephesians 6:12)
You wake me everyday around three or four
As to you I pray and kneel down before
Making me over down to the core
In my life you open a shut door
You're all consuming power I can't ignore
Send your rain down, I just want more and more

References

The Holy Bible: <u>Old and New Testaments In the King James Version.</u> *(1976). Nashville: Thomas Nelson Publishers*

Acknowledgements

I would like to thank God first, for the gift of expression through words, and for the many blessing that he has bestowed upon me. Never did I think that He would give me writings to flow continuously that I'm already working on my second book. I would like to say thank you to Pastor Shirley Nelson and Assistant Pastor Gail Gethers, for their astound teachings, and leadership while attending "MTOP Ministry". Lastly, I would like to say thank you to my family, friends, and associates that have supported, and inspired me throughout the years.

Author Autobiography

It has been a time in life that reading was her escape from going to bed earlier as writing has become her escape, and outward expression. Some say that Chandler's just a thinker, but life's experiences, with love, hurt, pain, downfalls, transitions, and spiritual growth has inspired her to write this book. Chandler possesses an Associates of Science, Bachelors of Science Accounting , and Masters of Science in Mental Health Counseling.

In poetry, Chandler takes you through life's journeys its ups, and downs, focused to motivate, inspire through life's situations with love, relationships, friendship, leading the way to spirituality, and spiritual growth. You wouldn't have to meet her to know her personality, or how ones emotions are at given times, it's shown in her poetry. In "Lesson

Learned" you can feel betrayal, In "Encouraging & Thinking" she speaks of her spiritual growth and desires, showing the transition from the world to Christianity. Her poetry reminds readers that though life can engulf you there is light at the end of the tunnel.

Chandler resides in North Carolina while reading has always been one of her joys in life most favorite as a little girl writing poetry and songs her spoken passion. Poetry has been the voice of life's ups and downs; and brought much comfort to family, and friends. In Chandler's poems you will hear the emotional, heartache, love, and pain from life's struggles to a change, and spiritual gain. On the contrary poetry also includes some poems inspired by family friends.

Find out more about author, events, on www.smchandler.com